Bullying Is a Pain in the Brain

by Trevor Romain

Illustrated by Steve Mark

free spirit
PUBLISHING®

Library of Congress Cataloging-in-Publication Data
Names: Romain, Trevor. | Mark, Steve, illustrator.
Title: Bullying is a pain in the brain / written by Trevor Romain ; illustrated by Steve Mark.
Other titles: Bullies are a pain in the brain.
Description: Revised & Updated Edition. | Golden Valley : Free Spirit Publishing, 2016. | Series: Laugh & Learn series | Description based on print version record and CIP data provided by publisher; resource not viewed.
Identifiers: LCCN 2015042303 (print) | LCCN 2015040918 (ebook) | ISBN 9781631980770 (Web pdf) | ISBN 9781631980787 (epub) | ISBN 9781631980657 (paperback) | ISBN 1631980653
Subjects: LCSH: Bullying—Juvenile humor. | CYAC: Bullying. | Bullies. | BISAC: JUVENILE NONFICTION / Social Issues / Bullying. | JUVENILE NONFICTION / Social Issues / Self-Esteem & Self-Reliance. | JUVENILE NONFICTION / Social Issues / Emotions & Feelings.
Classification: LCC BF637.B85 (print) | LCC BF637.B85 R66 2016 (ebook) | DDC 302.34/3—dc23
LC record available at http://lccn.loc.gov/2015042303

Free Spirit Publishing does not have control over or assume responsibility for author or third-party websites and their content. At the time of this book's publication, all facts and figures cited within are the most current available. All telephone numbers, addresses, and website URLs are accurate and active; all publications, organizations, websites, and other resources exist as described in this book; and all have been verified as of November 2015. If you find an error or believe that a resource listed here is not as described, please contact Free Spirit Publishing. Parents, teachers, and other adults: We strongly urge you to monitor children's use of the Internet.

Reading Level Grade 5; Interest Level Ages 8–13;
Fountas & Pinnell Guided Reading Level T

Edited by Elizabeth Verdick and Eric Braun
Designed by Emily Dyer

10 9 8 7 6 5 4 3 2 1
Printed in China
R18860116

Free Spirit Publishing Inc.
6325 Sandburg Road, Suite 100
Golden Valley, MN 55427-3674
(612) 338-2068
help4kids@freespirit.com
www.freespirit.com

FSC
www.fsc.org
MIX
Paper from
responsible sources
FSC® C101537

Free Spirit offers competitive pricing.
Contact edsales@freespirit.com for pricing information on
multiple quantity purchases.

Dedication

Dedicated to my late grandfather Teddy Tanchel, the best hugger in the world.

Acknowledgments

I would like to thank Judy Galbraith, Margie Lisovskis, Elizabeth Verdick, Eric Braun, and the entire Free Spirit crew who not only encouraged me to find my self-help wings but helped me soar.

A big thank you to all educators, especially teachers and special education teachers. As a kid with dyslexia and ADHD, I would not have reached my dreams if it weren't for you.

Contents

Chapter 1

Do you Have a Problem with Bullying?

The alarm clock buzzes and you slowly crawl out of bed. Another school day, and you're miserable. For the past few weeks, a kid in your class has been picking on you, pushing you when the teacher isn't looking, calling you "Dog Breath" (or worse), putting your photo on social media with embarrassing captions, and generally getting on your nerves. You didn't do anything to provoke this behavior, and you're wondering why he has chosen *you* for a target.

You get your lunch money from your mom and hide it in your shoe, hoping that kid won't try to take your money today. Then you go wait for the school bus. When it pulls up, you see him staring out at you from the back of the bus with a mean grin. "Uh-oh," you think. "How am I supposed to handle this today?"

Does any of this sound familiar?

If you're trying to cope with a bullying problem, here's the first thing you need to know:

You're not alone.

Everyone has been bullied at some point. Other kids in your school or neighborhood are probably dealing with bullying problems similar to yours. The trouble is, a lot of times people keep bullying a secret. They feel ashamed or scared to talk about what's really happening. They think that if they ignore the situation, it will go away.

(It won't.)

Here's the second thing you need to know about your bullying problem:

It's not your fault.

You're not doing the bullying. Someone else is. You didn't ask to be bullied. Someone else decided to bully you. Was it something you did? Something you said? Is it because of how you look or where you live or what you wear or any other reason you can possibly think of?

(Nope.)

What Is Bullying, Anyway?

According to experts on bullying, bullying is when someone treats another person in a mean or unwanted way, over and over. It can be:

physical, like hitting, tripping, pinching, poking, shoving, or giving wet willies

verbal, like making fun of the way people look or act, making fun of their religion or race, calling people mean names, or laughing at people

relational, like leaving someone out on purpose, spreading gossip or rumors about somebody, or telling people not to hang out with someone

Bullying done on electronic technology such as phones or computers is **cyberbullying.**

In other words: People who bully have serious problems. They like to hurt and frighten others they see as smaller or weaker. Experts tell us that people who bully like to be in control. By controlling you, they feel strong and superior. And you feel puny, afraid—and angry.

Some people bully to get attention. They believe that bullying is a way to be popular and a good way to get what they want. By bullying, they try to make themselves feel more important or powerful.

Some people come from families where there is a lot of fighting and yelling and anger. It may seem weird, but they believe that pushing people around, being angry, and messing with others is a normal way to behave. Many people who bully copy what they have seen others do, and often they've been bullied themselves. You'll see later in this book why reporting bullying may help a person like this realize that this kind of behavior is NOT normal or acceptable.

Bullying happens everywhere—in small communities, towns, big cities, playgrounds, neighborhoods, malls, parks, on the streets, online, and anywhere else people gather. Most of all, bullying happens in schools. It may be happening right next to you in class.

People who bully come in all shapes and sizes. Boys can bully, and so can girls. Adults can bully, too. Bullying has been around for centuries. In fact, people have been bothering, pestering, hurting, and troubling others for too long.

The good News is, bullying can be stopped.

This book will help you understand why some people bully and how you can deal with them. You'll read about becoming **"Bully-Proof,"** stopping people from hurting others, and getting help in dangerous situations. If you're the one doing the bullying, this book can also help you. You'll see that you *can* get along with others and feel good about yourself without making other people's lives a complete misery. And you can also learn to deal with bullying in *your* life.

Young people have a right to feel safe, secure, and protected at school and in their communities. If you don't feel safe, reading this book can be the first step toward changing that.

QUICK QUIZ

Which of these words describe someone who bullies?

young

OLD

smart

not so

FAT

average

thin

muscular

not so muscular

TALL

smart

short

large

small

The answer? All of the above!

Chapter 2

Why Bullying Is Such a Pain

People who bully can be big or little, tall or short, husky or skinny, brainy or dumb. You can't always identify them by their looks. But there's one thing they have in common: They like to be in charge. The more they drain the self-esteem of others, the better they feel.

You might even say they are Self-Esteem Vampires.

PEOPLE ARE MORE THAN LABELS

Calling people names is mean and unfair—even calling someone a bully. Labeling someone with a name like that can make it seem like that's all he or she is: a bully. But people are much more than one thing, and people can change. Even someone who steals your lunch money and embarrasses you on the bus can learn to treat people better. That's why it's best never to call someone a name like "bully." When we use labels like that, we make it easier to see the person as just a label—and not the person inside.

Even labels that don't seem very mean, like "jock," "cat person," "music lover," or "movie buff," can limit the way we see a person. People use these labels all the time, but labels don't show who you really are. It would take a **billion** labels to truly describe you.

Bullying harms people in many different ways—physically, mentally, and emotionally. These are the things kids who bully do best: hit, punch, kick, tease, push, pull, pester, brag, taunt, harass, play mind games, frighten, heckle, insult, annoy, gossip, bother, hurt, threaten, torment, ridicule, trip, pinch, act violent, and intimidate. They can be experts at excluding kids from groups or activities, spreading lies and rumors online, and making kids do things they don't want to do.

Imagine listing those "skills" on your résumé when you're looking for a job. Picture someone at a job interview:

Here's what people who bully aren't so good at: making friends, being kind, caring about people, sharing, and getting along with others. Often, these kids come from homes where the parents yell a lot or use physical force to make their kids behave. As a result, they have a lot of anger inside them.

What do these kids do with their anger? They take it out on the people (or pets) around them. They choose the people they pick on *verrrry* carefully. Usually they bully kids who aren't likely to defend themselves.

If you know kids who bully a lot, give them plenty of space, because they lose their temper quickly. If you can smell their breath, you're too close! Being nearby when they lose their temper is like being too close to a water fountain when someone turns it on.

LOOK OUT!

Chapter 3

What You Can Do About Bullying

Kids bully people who appear anxious, sensitive, quiet, or cautious. Like ants are attracted to candy, these kids are drawn to people who are somewhat shy. They might also pick on those who are younger or physically smaller.

So, what's your best defense?

A **DISGUISE**, you say . . . ?

Look Confident

No, you don't have to wear a disguise or change who you are just because someone has decided to bother you. Instead, work on appearing more sure of yourself. Stand up straight, look people in the eye, talk with a firm voice, and hold your head high. If you *act* more confident, you'll soon start to *feel* more confident.

Not Confident

head drooping

downcast eyes

poor posture

knees knocking

Confident

head held high

confident smile

thumbs-up sign

good posture

People bully because they love power. The more power they get, the more they want. Kids who bully think they've hit the jackpot when they make you cry. Don't reward them with tears. Instead, stay as calm as you can and walk away with confidence.

Speak Up

Many kids who bully are very competitive. They hate to lose at sports, games, races—or *anything*. To make sure they win, they might play dirty. They cheat, or they beat up anyone who stands in their way. Some kids even consider popularity a competition. They embarrass or spread rumors about kids so people won't like them.

If someone is cheating or playing dirty, try speaking up. Often, if you or someone else speaks up, other kids will agree with you. Nobody likes playing with a cheater.

Dude, quit that. We're trying to have fun.

Hey, that's cheating and it's ruining the game. Knock it off!

Tell an Adult

If you speak up and the other kid keeps cheating, it might be time to get an adult involved like a teacher or parent. (If you're afraid that the other kids will make fun of you for speaking up, you can talk to the grown-up in charge quietly or even tell the adult later.)

If no adults are around, and you are not enjoying the game or if you feel uncomfortable or threatened, it may be best to stop playing and remove yourself from the situation.

Some kids demand "payment" from the people they bully.

They get rich quick from taking other people's belongings. Sometimes they even destroy or vandalize other people's property.

Tell an adult if someone has stolen from you, threatened you, or damaged something belonging to you. Stealing is against the law and is a crime even if the person doing it is a schoolkid.

How to Deal with Bullying by the Bunch

What is worse than a kid who bullies? A group who bullies. What do you call a group who bullies? A gang. Gangs are dangerous. Because the gang members outnumber you, they can be even more intimidating. The safest thing to do is *avoid gangs altogether*. Gang members may try to persuade you to join them. Don't believe that you'll be more cool, popular, or tough by belonging to a gang. Many gang members end up in jail, in the hospital, or dead.

Some gangs carry weapons, making them even more dangerous. What should you do if you see someone who has a gun or knife? Leave the area quickly and quietly. Don't threaten, ignore, attack, or provoke the person. Once you're in a safe place, immediately tell an adult about the weapon. You can tell a parent, teacher, school counselor, principal, or police officer.

If a person or a gang is targeting you, take the long way home to avoid the path of the people bothering you.

Take the **EXTRA** long way home, if necessary.*

*Even better, find a friend to walk home with you. Or ask your mom or dad to pick you up.

If the person or gang still comes after you, RUN! (You might look a bit foolish running down the street like a maniac, but you will look *alive*.)

RUN home, if it's close enough to run to.

RUN to a group of people, if there's one nearby.

RUN to a neighbor's home.

Find out if there's a block parent program in your neighborhood. Learn where it is. If your neighborhood doesn't have one, tell your parents. Ask if they can work with your neighbors or police department to start one.

What Being Bullied Feels Like—and How to Change It

Sometimes a kid or a group of kids will make your life miserable by:

threatening or insulting you

holding you down

making jokes about you

purposely ignoring you in a mean way

getting others to exclude you

giving you dirty looks

calling you names

making unfriendly gestures

spreading rumors about you

posting nasty comments or pictures online

Bullying can be a real pain, because the people who do it often see another person's success as their own failure. Then they become jealous and angry, and they want to hurt the person who's succeeding.

You probably feel scared, sad, angry, alone, and frustrated when you're being bullied. That's exactly how the kid who's bullying *wants* you to feel! Don't let bullying take away your self-esteem. Find your strengths and achieve your goals. That way, no matter how hard someone tries to tear down your self-esteem, you'll keep believing in yourself.

You'll be **Bully-Proof!**

DO YOU BULLY YOURSELF?

Believe it or not, people can actually bully *themselves*. They do this by telling themselves, "I'm no good," or "I'm stupid," or "I can't do anything right." They make *themselves* feel scared, sad, angry, alone, and frustrated.

If you're bullying yourself, CUT IT OUT. What can you do instead? Here are two ideas:

1 Start telling yourself, "I'm a strong person," "I'm smart," "I can do it."

2 Do your best! If there's something you want to achieve and you really try, you'll probably succeed. (Even if you don't, you'll feel good that you gave it your best shot.)

If you want to do better on spelling tests, study harder. If you want to pitch for your softball team, practice! Believe in yourself, and you give yourself a great chance to succeed.

Many kids have found that being with friends is a great way to deal with bullying. So make friends—lots of them! Kids who bully can't stand groups of happy, smiling, friendly people. You can make friends by joining a club or participating in group activities like sports, music, or acting. Another great way to make friends is to invite others to do things—even just to sit with you at lunch. If someone is being picked on, stick up for that person.

Smiling helps, too!

Have you ever wondered what friends really are for (besides being homework helpers, frog-hunting partners, secret keepers, and text message exchangers)?

Here's what: Friends are for sticking by you in tough times. Tell your friends if you're being bullied. You are less likely to be bullied if you're **surrounded by your buddies.** Plus, your friends could even stick up for you by saying, "We don't like the way you treat our friend," or, "We don't like the way you're acting. Stop it!"

Chapter 4

Five Myths About Bullying

MYTH #1 — People who bully have low self-esteem, which is why they pick on other people.

Fact: Some studies have shown that many people who bully actually have *high* self-esteem. But they want to feel even *more* powerful and in control.

 Only boys bully.

Fact: Girls bully, too. All kinds of kids bully. Sometimes girls will pick on girls and boys will pick on boys. And girls will sometimes pick on boys, and boys will sometimes pick on girls.

MYTH #3 Getting bullied is a normal part of growing up.

Fact: What's "normal" about feeling afraid to go to school? Or putting up with threats or physical abuse? This myth is just an excuse for bad behavior. Plus it helps create a "code of silence" about bullying. If you think bullying is "normal," you don't say anything about it, and you don't do anything about it. Nobody else does, either. Meanwhile, kids keep on bullying.

The best way to handle bullying is by getting even or fighting back.

Fact: Sometimes bullying is a life-or-death situation. If you try to get even with someone who's bullying you or defend yourself using physical force or a weapon, things will only get worse. A person who feels cornered or provoked is likely to come after you again. If a weapon is involved, *you* may be the one who ends up getting hurt.

MYTH #5

If you ignore bullying, it will stop.

Fact: Some people who bully may get *more* angry if you ignore them (after all, bullying can be their way of getting attention). They may keep provoking you just to get some kind of reaction.

So, what in the world are you supposed to do when you're bullied? Take a deep breath, look the other person in the eye, and say in your firmest, most confident voice:

"Leave me alone, I don't like what you're doing."

OR...

"Don't do that. I don't like it."

OR...

"I'll report you if you don't stop bothering me."

OR...

"Quit it."

Then Walk Away.

Because it isn't easy to communicate with someone who's being mean, you might want to rehearse what you'll say. At home, stand in front of a mirror and pretend you're talking to the person. Speak clearly and firmly. Stand tall and show confidence. Practice saying the words until you feel sure of yourself.

You can even ask a family member or friend to help out by role-playing. That person would play the kid who's bullying you, and you would play yourself. You'll soon get comfortable looking someone in the eye and telling that person to leave you alone.

If the person keeps bothering you, remember this advice:

You can yell, "Take your hands off me!" or "You're hurting me!" or "Leave me alone!" Shouting will probably take the kid by surprise, and you'll have a chance to quickly walk away. If you're in a crowded place, other people will most likely turn and look. This may make the kid who's bullying feel uncomfortable and decide to go away.

Chapter 5

Bringing Bullying Out in the Open

Don't be afraid to tell an adult if you're being bullied. You might feel more comfortable talking to the adult in private, so nobody can see or hear you. You are NOT tattling if you report someone who's hurting you.

Here are some adults who can help you:

a parent

a relative

your teacher

a school counselor

your principal

a police officer

By reporting bullying, you're helping yourself *and* others. Think of all the other kids who get picked on each day. They'll be grateful that you put a stop to the problem. And believe it or not, you might actually help the person who's bullying! With some guidance, people who shame, hurt, and embarrass others can learn to make friends and solve their problems without using violence and intimidation.

Sadly, sometimes adults bully, too. If a grown-up is bullying you, it's not your fault. Talk about the problem with an adult you trust. A parent, teacher, principal, or coach can help keep you safe.

Ask your teacher or school counselor to hold a bullying-prevention workshop. During the workshop, the class can talk about what bullying is, what causes it, and how to stop it. You could also suggest role-playing exercises, with some students acting like they're bullying and others being bullied. Practice the different strategies for dealing with bullying. It can be very helpful to deal with bullying problems in a group setting.

Does your school have a peer mediation program? Peer mediators are students in your school who have been trained to help solve disputes between other students.

A **mediator**, or go-between, might be able to help the kids who are bullying and the kids who are being bullied make peace. (If the problem is too serious, however, adult help is needed.)

The benefit of bringing bullying problems out in the open is that the one who's bullying is no longer in control. It won't be as easy for someone to pick on you or other students because everyone will have a better understanding of how to make him stop. And when teachers and school officials are aware of bullying, they can find ways to help those who do it change their behavior.

Chapter 6

Do's and Don'ts for Dealing with Bullying

When someone teases you about your looks, your clothes, your grades, or anything else...

DO stick up for yourself. Say:

"Hmm... thanks for the advice. I'll consider it."

OR...

"You have your opinion, I have mine."

OR...

"You can think what you want. But I'm happy with the way I am."

Try not to take it personally. The teasing doesn't really have anything to do with *you*. The person doing it is looking for power and control.

DON'T begin to gag and gasp for air, clutch your throat and make gurgling noises, fall to the floor choking and then, when the kid asks what's wrong with you, tell her she's irritating you to death. If you try this crazy stunt, you'll only make things worse. Taunting someone back is like teasing a vicious dog. (You might end up sitting on an ice pack to soothe the spot where the dog nipped your behind.)

When someone threatens you . . .

DO use your best judgment and follow your instincts. For example: If someone says he'll punch your lights out if you don't give him your lunch money, you might say, "I don't want to give you my money. And if you try to force me, I'll report you to the principal." But what if you and he are the only two people in the hallway and you're about to get beat up? Give him your money. Then tell an adult.

DON'T drop to your knees and whine, "Here, take my lunch money! Take all of it! Take my backpack, too! I'll do anything you want . . . just don't hurt me! Please, please, please!"

Kids who bully love it when their victims beg for mercy. It makes them want to come back for more.

When someone calls you names . . .

DO try your best not to pay attention to what the kid is saying. Walk away (try whistling the National Anthem to block out the mean noise). No matter what the kid says, you're not a dork, wimp, teacher's pet, dummy, loser, crybaby, jerk-face, or knucklehead. And anything that's said about your race, family, gender, religion, or national heritage is only said to hurt you or push your buttons for a reaction.

DON'T break down in tears, think "I really *am* a loser," go home and pull the bed covers over your head, stop spending time with your friends, or lose interest in your hobbies because you think you're no good. Remember, kids who bully love to get under your skin. If you let their mean words hurt you, you'll be giving them what they want.

When someone spreads rumors about you or says mean things online . . .

DO talk to the person about what she said. Maybe she thought it was just a joke and didn't know how much it hurt you. Talking can get the person to stop spreading hurtful words about you.

If the person refuses to stop, report the bullying to an adult. A teacher, principal, or parent can help put an end to it. Hurting people by spreading mean things about them is a form of harassment and may even be against the law in your area.

DON'T try to get revenge by making a mean website about the person who has been bullying you. Don't start rumors about anyone, and don't use social media to embarrass or hurt someone. If you do that, *you* are harassing—and you can get into trouble.

You can read a lot more about this very ugly thing called cyberbullying in the next chapter.

When someone picks a fight with you . . .

DO get away as fast as you can, and tell an adult. Tell your teacher, your mom or dad, your principal, or another adult nearby. It takes two to fight. If you refuse to take part, you're less likely to get hurt.

DON'T put up your dukes and say, "I could beat you up with one hand tied behind my back." (This is an invitation to give the tooth fairy a lot of work.) If you get into a fight, you have nothing to gain and everything to lose. Chances are, someone who picks a fight with you has had a lot more practice using her fists. And if you get caught fighting on school grounds, both of you will get into trouble, no matter who started it.

When you see someone who bullies coming toward you . . .

DO get out of his way! Step aside, join your friends, strike up a conversation with someone nearby, or walk toward a crowded place. This way, the person can't get you alone.

DON'T pick your nose and pretend you're about to eat it, in the hope that he will throw up with disgust and leave you in peace.

Did you know that many kids who bully are budding actors? They spend a lot of time rehearsing their clever lines, such as:

I'M going to teach you a lesson you'll never forget.

You're dead, kid.

I'M gonna rearrange your face.

You would think they were up for an Academy Award!

Eat my fist!

Learning self-defense is a good way to protect yourself and increase your self-confidence. You might try taking a karate class. In karate, you'll find out how to defend yourself, and you'll gain the confidence *not* to fight. (And, if you wear your black belt to school, other kids will get the message!)

Sometimes humor can help ease a problem. If someone threatens to beat you up, you might say, "Hey, I'll save you the time and trouble. I'll go home right now and beat myself up. That way, your hands won't get hurt." He may laugh and decide to leave you alone.

(**CAUTION:** Be sure your joke isn't directed at the other kid. He might think you're making fun of him.)

Sometimes an "I-message" can cool things down. For example: If someone calls you a big dork, don't say, "You're mean!" or worse, "You're a jerk!" That's a "you-message" and puts the other person on the defensive. It can make him act even meaner or get angrier.

An I-message says what *you* feel or what *you* plan to do.

"I don't like it when you call me that, because it really annoys me. Besides, I am NOT a big dork, as anyone can plainly see."

"I'm not going to listen to insults."

"I don't really care if some people think I'm a dork."

When someone is bullying other kids . . .

DO try to stand up for others. Maybe your friend is being bullied. Or maybe it's happening to someone you don't even know. Either way, just saying something might make it stop. When someone bullies, the person doesn't expect anybody to say anything. Speaking up by saying "Hey, leave him alone!" can be a big surprise for people who bully. Sometimes that's enough to make them stop. Sometimes, other kids might join you in standing up to bullying. When that happens, you have a chance to make a big change in your classroom—and even your whole school!

One of the most important things you can do is be kind to kids who are being bullied. Invite them to hang out with you. Sit with them on the bus or at lunch. Let them know they are not alone.

DON'T say, "Whew, glad it's not *me* being picked on," and walk away thanking your lucky stars.

The people who witness bullying are called bystanders. When **bystanders** stand together, they can make big changes. It's only when people act like bullying is okay that it keeps going on. And on, and on, and on.

(And on!)

You can do even more to help change a bullying culture. Get involved in a bullying-prevention program or a safety program at your school. If there isn't one, talk to a teacher or principal about starting one. Make posters about bullying, or write a blog or letter to the editor of a local newspaper. Write a story for

your school newspaper or website. Use social media to talk about positive things that happen at your school. Want to catch a kid who's being mean off guard? **Try making friends with him!**

Many kids bully others because they are dealing with certain social problems. They might have trouble making friends, or feel really bad about themselves, or they have problems at home. It may seem weird, but for some kids it's easier to bully others than it is to deal with their emotions and try to solve their problems.

You can set a good example for these kids. You and other students might be able to inspire someone to change her bullying behavior simply by being friendly and helping her feel better about herself.

Chapter 7

What About Cyberbullying?

Bad News . . .

People have more ways than just words and physical force to bully others. They can also use their cell phones, tablets, and computers.

No, they don't use these devices as weapons to throw at people. They use them to embarrass, threaten, humiliate, or shame people.

They might put hurtful or embarrassing photographs, videos, information, text messages, or Web posts online. They might do this with social media like Instagram or on websites. They might use text messages and email.

This type of bullying is called cyberbullying.

Quick, Easy, and Painful

Bullying online is happening more and more because it's easier to do than other types of bullying. Plus, kids can do it anywhere—at home, in school, and anywhere else people go online. Someone might not have the courage to call you a name to your face. But posting a rude message online just takes a few clicks.

These messages and images are even easier to spread—and they can spread *fast*. As soon as one person forwards a message or "likes" a post, the audience grows. The pain and embarrassment multiplies.

Meanwhile, the person who started it all gets to hide behind a computer or phone.

Just like other forms of bullying, cyberbullying can stress you out. It can make you grumpy, anxious, sad, and depressed. Being targeted by cyberbullying can be scary and lonely.

If you ever feel any of these feelings because of something you see online or in a text, please tell a trusted grown-up right away.

And here's the Good News:

REPORTING REALLY DOES HELP!

Just like other kinds of bullying, there's a lot you can do to stop it from happening to you—AND others. Read on to learn how.

Answers to Some Tricky Cyberbullying Questions

Holy emojis, cyberbullying can be confusing! Can you really do anything about the bullying that happens online?

If you're confused or uncertain about cyberbullying, try not to worry. Read through these common questions to get some helpful answers.

Question

Sometimes it's hard to tell online if someone is joking or not. How do you know?

Answer: Bullying involves repeated insults and hurtful comments that go beyond teasing or words said in anger. If it happens more than once, that's bullying. If you ask someone to stop and she doesn't, that's bullying.

Question

What should I do if people have said stuff about me online and it makes me sad and embarrassed and afraid?

Answer: Tell an adult right away. Bullying often gets worse once it has started. Parents, schools, and sometimes law enforcement need to know about cyberbullying.

It's also important to block the person who is cyberbullying you. On social media, this can be easy. If you receive mean messages or images, don't reply and don't forward them. Keep them as evidence.

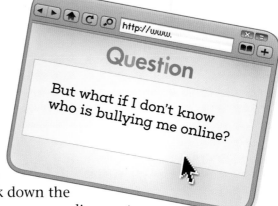

Question

But what if I don't know who is bullying me online?

Answer:
Police and online experts often can track down the authors of anonymous online posts.
So please don't hesitate to tell a trusted adult if you (or someone you know) is being bullied, harassed, or teased in a way that hurts.

Question

What if friends are being mean and hurtful online? Is it okay for them to do that?

Answer: It's not okay for **anyone**, whether they're a friend or not, to bully you. If something a friend or group of friends does online upsets you, be sure to let them know that you are not happy with what they have said about you. If they say it's just a joke, tell them it's not a joke to you. If it continues, tell an adult.

If you can't trust your friend to treat you fairly and with respect, you might have to end the friendship. Friendship does not give people permission to treat you badly.

Question

How can I prevent people from cyberbullying me?

Answer:

To make it harder for people to bully you online:

- Don't share any of your passwords with anyone except your parents—not even with your BFF.

- Always think carefully about what you post. Could it be misunderstood by someone? Would you be embarrassed if the wrong person saw it? Anything that goes online or that is shared by text message or social media can stay online forever. Even if you take it down, it may already be on other people's computers or phones.

- Only use social media if you are old enough (most sites require users to be 13) and if you have your parent's permission. If you do have social media accounts, use your privacy settings. Only become "friends" with people you know and trust. Think about who can see what you post. Block anyone who cyberbullies. (You can learn about blocking and other privacy settings under a site's "Terms of Service" or "Privacy Policy." Ask an adult if you need help.)

ALERT!
Major warning.

Do not ignore this: It is against the law in most states to harass people. Cyberbullying is a form of harassment. The police may get involved if anyone makes mean or threatening comments to others online.

Question

What if I see cyberbullying but it's not directed at me? Isn't the safest thing to mind my own business?

Answer: Just like all other kinds of bullying, cyberbullying is everyone's problem. If you help stop it from happening, everyone is happier—including you!

- Don't forward mean messages or pictures.

- Don't participate in mean polls, chats, or other things where people are ganging up on someone online.

- Do tell friends who cyberbully that it is wrong.

- Do stick up for friends online.

Question

What if the bullying makes me so angry that I just want to hurt them back?

Answer: It's normal to get angry and upset when someone tries to hurt you, but trying to get revenge often makes it worse. If you cyberbully someone back, you can get in trouble. Instead, take a break and get off your phone or computer for a while. Don't respond or engage with the bullying. Responding to people who are bullying you will give them power over you, just like a marionette puppet. Don't let them pull your strings. By not responding, you keep the power.

Question

What happens if I tell an adult about being bullied and he doesn't do anything about it?

Answer: That is a very important question. DO NOT stop asking for support if one person is unable or unwilling to help you.

Create a `support team` for yourself. Draw an outline of your hand on a piece of paper, and on top of each finger write down the name of a grown-up who loves and cares about you. These five people will be your team. Your starting five.

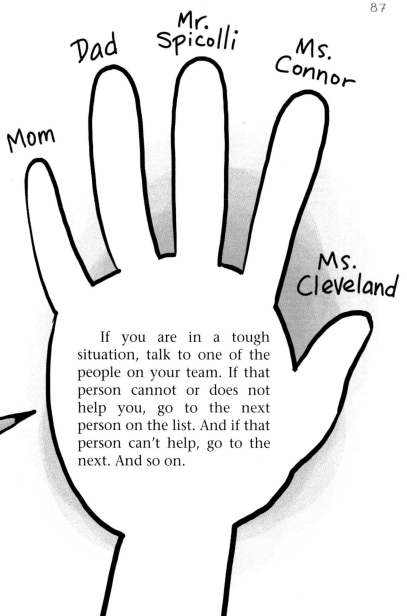

Mom

Dad

Mr. Spicolli

Ms. Connor

Ms. Cleveland

If you are in a tough situation, talk to one of the people on your team. If that person cannot or does not help you, go to the next person on the list. And if that person can't help, go to the next. And so on.

Chapter 8

Are you Bullying?

Are you wondering if you've been bullying? Here's a quick way to tell. Look over the following list. If you answer "yes" to one or two of these questions, you may be on your way to bullying. If you answered "yes" to three or more of these questions, you probably *are* bullying, and you need to find ways to change your behavior.

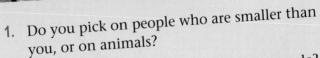

1. Do you pick on people who are smaller than you, or on animals?

2. Do you like to tease and taunt other people?

3. If you tease people, do you like to see them get upset?

4. Do you think it's funny when other people make mistakes?

5. Do you like to take or destroy other people's belongings?

6. Do you want other students to think you're the toughest kid in school?

7. Do you get angry a lot and stay angry for a long time?

8. Do you blame other people for things that go wrong in your life?

9. Do you like to get revenge on people who hurt you?

10. Do you try to control the people you hang out with?

11. Do you laugh when other kids get hurt or embarrassed online?

12. Do you send mean text messages or social media posts?

13. When you play a game or sport, do you always have to be the winner?

14. If you lose at something, do you worry about what other people will think of you?

15. Do you get angry or jealous when someone else succeeds?

Uh-oh! Did you just find out that you've been acting like a bully? Or maybe the list describes someone else you know—your brother or sister, or your best friend.

The good news is: Anyone can get help dealing with their feelings, getting along with other people, and making friends. Parents, teachers, school counselors, and other adults can all give this kind of help. Just ask.

One thing people who bully have in common with the people they target is ANGER. They take out their anger on their targets—the people they bully. Then their targets feel angry because of the way they've been treated.

The next time anger boils up inside you, try dealing with it positively. Take a few deep breaths, count backward until you feel more relaxed, imagine a peaceful place, pet your dog, think about things that make you feel good, or talk to someone about your anger.

Chapter 9

Be Bully-Free

Everybody, everywhere has been bullied at some point in their lives. Even people who bully have been bullied! (Which is one reason why they act the way they do.)

But that doesn't mean bullying is okay. Or that you should suffer in silence. Or that you should bully. What will *you* do the next time someone bullies you? Think about it. Make a plan. Be ready to speak up, walk away, or run away.

Bullying is a pain in the brain. But it doesn't have to give *you* a permanent headache.

A Message for Teachers and Parents

Most of us can recall a time when we've been bullied. But today bullying is more serious. Kids have taken desperate measures, such as using a gun in self-defense or committing suicide, to deal with their bullying problems. Many children are afraid to go to school. When they do, they avoid areas perceived as dangerous, such as restrooms and secluded hallways.

Since this book first came out in 1997, people have become much more aware of the dangers of bullying. New laws protect kids from bullying based on race, sex, and ability. Many schools have antiviolence and conflict-resolution programs that help the kids involved in bullying find ways to get along. We know that bystanders have the most power to end bullying—even more than adults—and many schools are working to empower them to do just that.

It's important to implement system-wide efforts and strategies to continue to curb bullying. For example, targets need to feel confident that if they report a bullying problem to school officials, something will be done. Everyone needs to understand that bullying behavior won't be tolerated.

If you're a teacher, you can take steps to curb bullying in your classroom and beyond:

1. Find out how common bullying is in your school. Create and distribute an anonymous questionnaire, or talk privately with other teachers, your students, and their parents.

2. Set firm rules against bullying in your classroom. Make sure everyone sees and knows the rules.

3. Be aware of incidents of aggression that take place in the restrooms, on the playground, in the lunchroom, and in hallways. Monitor these areas to ensure a safer school environment.

4. Keep a written record of bullying incidents, including the names, dates, times, and circumstances. Submit the reports to the principal.

5. Give students a chance to talk about bullying and its effects. Hold workshops or class discussions.

6. Get administrators and parents involved in reinforcing good behavior and supporting victims of bullying.

7. As much as possible, monitor computer use in your class, and pay attention to what kids are doing on their devices.

8. Encourage everyone to stand up to bullying, even kids who are not directly involved. Teach kids that bystanders can stop and prevent bullying when they stand together.

If you're a parent, you may not be aware that your child is being bullied. Many kids are afraid to let an adult know what's happening. They feel embarrassed and think they have to handle the situation on their own. Have you noticed any of the following signs in your child?

- Skips school or is often too sick to go to school
- Has unexplained bruises
- Has experienced a slip in grades
- Is reluctant to talk about school
- Hides social media profiles from you, or worries a lot about what kids are saying online
- Is missing belongings
- Suddenly has fewer friends (or no friends)

- Frequently requests lunch money to replace "lost" money

- Comes home in dirty clothes (from fights)

If you see a few or several of these signs, your child might be having trouble with bullying. Here's what you can do if your child is being bullied:

1. Talk with your child, letting him or her know that you understand and care.

2. Get in touch with your child's teacher or with school officials to inform them of the situation. Do this after school, by phone, or in an email to protect your child's privacy and to make sure that other kids don't find out. Keep written accounts of the bullying incidents and the times when you've talked with school staff members about the problem.

3. Teach your child the skills needed to resolve a bullying situation. Throughout this book, you'll find several ideas you can role-play and practice with your child. "Fighting back" or "ignoring the situation" aren't solutions. Instead, your child needs to be verbally assertive and have the confidence to seek the help of an adult.

If you suspect that your child is the one doing the bullying, try some of these options:

- Talk to your child about the reasons behind the bullying. Reassure your child that you still love him or her.

- Consider family counseling to determine the cause of the problem. Your child may need help learning to manage anger and to resolve conflicts peacefully.

- Help your child understand the differences between aggressive and assertive behaviors.

- Let your child's teacher know that your child is trying to stop bullying. The teacher may be helpful in setting goals and correcting bad behavior.

Share the resources on pages 98–99 with your students or your child, and work together to find solutions to the problem of bullying. Help your children help themselves!

On pages 100–101 are lists of resources for adults that can help you learn more about bullying and what to do about it.

Resources for Kids

Books

Confessions of a Former Bully by Trudy Ludwig (New York: Dragonfly Books, 2010). After Katie gets caught teasing a schoolmate, she's told to meet with the school counselor so she can right her wrong and learn to be a better friend. Told from the point of view of the kid who's bullying, it provides real-life tools for identifying and stopping relational aggression. Ages 8–12.

Nobody! A Story About Overcoming Bullying in School by Erin Frankel (Minneapolis: Free Spirit Publishing, 2015). Thomas feels like no matter what he does, he can't escape Kyle's persistent bullying. With support from friends, classmates, and adults, Thomas starts to feel more confident in himself and his hobbies, while Kyle learns the importance of kindness to others. Ages 5–9.

Speak Up and Get Along! Learn the Mighty Might, Thought Chop, and More Tools to Make Friends, Stop Teasing, and Feel Good About Yourself by Scott Cooper (Minneapolis: Free Spirit Publishing, 2005). Learn 21 strategies you can use to express yourself, build relationships, end arguments and fights, stop bullying, and beat unhappy feelings. Ages 8–12.

Stand Up for Yourself and Your Friends: Dealing with Bullies and Bossiness and Finding a Better Way by Patti Kelley Criswell (American Girl, 2009). This book teaches girls how to spot bullying and how to stand up and speak out against it. Quizzes, quotes from girls, and "what do you do?" scenarios present advice in an age-appropriate, digestible way. Ages 8 and up.

Stick Up for Yourself! Every Kid's Guide to Personal Power and Positive Self-Esteem by Gershen Kaufman, Lev Raphael, and Pamela Espeland (Minneapolis: Free Spirit Publishing, 1999).

This book tells you how to stick up for yourself with other kids, older siblings, even parents and teachers. It can help you feel better about yourself, stronger inside, and more in charge of your life. Ages 8–12.

Weird series by Erin Frankel (Minneapolis: Free Spirit Publishing, 2012). These three books tell the story of an ongoing case of bullying from three third graders' perspectives. Luisa describes being targeted by bullying in *Weird!* Jayla shares her experience as a bystander to bullying in *Dare!* And in *Tough!*, Sam speaks from the point of view of someone initiating bullying. Ages 5–9.

Websites

It's My Life
pbskids.org/itsmylife/friends
This PBS site is a resource for kids and teens across six topic "channels": Friends, Family, School, Body, Emotions, and Money. It's loaded with information, advice, and games. Click on "Friends" to find the section on "Bullies."

Kids Against Bullying
www.pacerkidsagainstbullying.org
At Pacer's Kids Against Bullying website, you can sign a petition against bullying, watch videos featuring teen celebrities, find out what other kids have to say about bullying, answer quizzes, and be inspired to take action.

SB Kids
www.stopbullying.gov/kids
This U.S. government site explains what bullying is, with a section on cyberbullying, and gives plenty of ideas for preventing and responding to bullying. It has games, kid videos, and a "Get Help Now" page where kids can find out what to do if they have a problem right now.

Resources for Adults....

Books

The Bully, the Bullied, and the Bystander: From Preschool to High School—How Parents and Teachers Can Help Break the Cycle of Violence by Barbara Coloroso (NY: HarperCollins, 2008). This book for parents, teachers, and counselors offers insights into all types of bullying behaviors, helps aid understanding of the roles of bystanders as well as direct participants in bullying, and suggests methods for dealing with bullying and affirming children's dignity.

Bullying and Cyberbullying: What Every Educator Needs to Know by Elizabeth Kandel Englander (Cambridge, MA: Harvard Education Press, 2013). Englander dispels pervasive myths and misconceptions about peer cruelty, bullying, and cyberbullying. Drawing on her own and others' research, she shows how educators can flag problematic behaviors and frame effective responses.

Bullying at School: What We Know and What We Can Do by Dan Olweus (Cambridge, MA: Blackwell Publishers, 1993). The classic book for parents, teachers, and school principals, it explains the causes and consequences of bullying, tells how to recognize if a child is being targeted or is bullying others, and details effective ways of counteracting and preventing bullying problems.

No Kidding About Bullying: 125 Ready-to-Use Activities to Help Kids Manage Anger, Resolve Conflicts, Build Empathy, and Get Along by Naomi Drew, M.A. (Minneapolis: Free Spirit Publishing, 2010). This book gives educators and youth leaders a diverse range of activities they can use to help kids in grades 3–6 build empathy, manage anger, and work out conflicts.

Websites

Coalition for Children
safechild.org
For parents and educators, this site provides information, resources, and programs that help protect children. They also provide expert witness and consulting services.

Committee for Children
www.cfchildren.org
Creators of the Second Step SEL program, this organization provides research-based social-emotional learning materials to help children succeed in school and in life. Contact them for a free list of products and services.

NCJRS Virtual Library
www.ncjrs.gov/Library.html
This component of the National Criminal Justice Reference Service offers materials addressing juvenile justice, crime prevention, violence prevention, children's rights, and more. Contact them to request a list of available materials.

Index

About the Author and Illustrator

When **Trevor Romain** was 12, his teacher told him he wasn't talented enough to do art. By accident, he found out 20 years later that he could draw. Since that lucky day, he has written and illustrated more than 50 books for children. His books have sold more than a million copies worldwide and have been published in 18 different languages. Trevor also travels to schools, hospitals, summer camps, and military bases throughout the world, delivering stand-up comedy with inspirational self-help messages to hundreds of thousands of school-age children.

Trevor, who is passionate about helping young people face and overcome tough challenges, has been the president of the American Childhood Cancer Organization and is well known for his work with the Make-A-Wish Foundation, the United Nations, UNICEF, USO, and the Comfort Crew for Military Kids, which he co-founded. He has performed on multiple USO tours, has visited and worked with former child soldiers and at refugee camps and orphanages, and has worked with the United Nations developing educational materials for children living in armed conflict areas.

Steve Mark is a freelance illustrator and a part-time puppeteer. He lives in Minnesota and is the father of three and the husband of one. Steve has illustrated several books in the Laugh & Learn series, including *Don't Behave Like You Live in a Cave* and *Siblings: You're Stuck with Each Other, So Stick Together*.

Free Spirit's
Laugh & Learn® Series

Solid information, a kid-centric point of view, and a sense of humor combine to make each book in our Laugh & Learn series an invaluable tool for getting through life's rough spots. For ages 8–13. *Softcover; 72–136 pp.; illust.; 5⅛" x 7"*

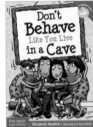

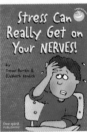